EVERYDAY GU
## MADE EA

# APPLE
# LOGIC PRO
# BASICS

This is a **FLAME TREE** book
First published 2015

**Publisher and Creative Director**: Nick Wells
**Project Editor**: Polly Prior
**Art Director and Layout Design**: Mike Spender
**Digital Design and Production**: Chris Herbert
**Copy Editor**: Anna Groves
**Technical Editor**: Ronan Macdonald
**Proofreader**: Sally Brigham
**Indexer**: Helen Snaith
**Screenshots**: Rusty Cutchin

**Special thanks to**: Gillian Whittaker

This edition first published 2015 by
**FLAME TREE PUBLISHING**
Crabtree Hall, Crabtree Lane
Fulham, London SW6 6TY
United Kingdom

www.flametreepublishing.com

15 17 19 18 16
1 3 5 7 9 10 8 6 4 2

© 2015 Flame Tree Publishing

ISBN 978-1-78361-400-4

A CIP record for this book is available from the British Library upon request.

Printed in China

All non-screenshot pictures are © Apogee 28 (l); and Apple 28 (r); and Roland 32; and Mackie 33; and PreSonus 34, 35; and Shutterstock and © the following photographers: pavelgr 1; Brisbane 3; graja 5; thelefty 6; wwwebmeister 7; Mark Burrows (Nottingham, UK) 8; Goodluz 15; iko 17; wavebreakmedia 18; Arina P Habich 24; Dragon Images 30, 45 and 88; Ruslan Absurdov 35; Jack Frog 41; Air Images 43; Jirsak 46; Balduk Andrey 47; Eugenio Marongiu 48; Soonios Pro 50; Sheftsoff Women Girls 51; joycedragan 53; Rommel Canlas 57, 72; bikeriderlondon 62, 91 and 101; Stokkete 64; Devin_Pavel 67; peresanz 68; Jaroslaw Brzychcy 70; Brian Goodman 80; ronstik 97; Chekunov Aleksandr 100; David Stuart Productions 103; Pavel Ignatov 104; Arman Zhenikeyev 105; TAGSTOCK1 107; Dennis Jacobsen 108; Jaromir Chalabala 115; Orla 118; BONNINSTUDIO 126. All other images courtesy of Flame Tree Publishing Ltd.

## EVERYDAY GUIDES
## MADE EASY

# APPLE
# LOGIC PRO
# BASICS

RUSTY CUTCHIN

FLAME TREE
PUBLISHING

# CONTENTS

Get started with a guide through the process of setting up Logic Pro on your Mac.

Explore the many ways of getting music into Logic Pro, including recording
your own audio and MIDI tracks with external hardware and using the internal
instruments and loops that come with the program.

Learn about the wide range of tools available for processing and shaping your sound,
editing your MIDI and audio tracks, adding video, and preparing the tracks for mixing.

Add the right effects and adjust the levels with Logic Pro's tools, using Logic's
extensive tools to make your final mix the best it can be.

Finalize your mix with the essential touches and get your track out to the world.

# SERIES FOREWORD

While the unstoppable rise of computer technology has left no area of the creative arts untouched, perhaps the most profoundly transformed of them all is music. From performance, composition and production to marketing, distribution and playback, the Apple Mac and Windows PC – and, more recently, their increasingly capable smartphone and tablet cousins – have given anyone, no matter what their budget, the ability to produce professional quality tracks in the comfort of their own home and put them online for the whole world to hear.

Virtual studios like Logic Pro and Pro Tools (and the software instruments and effects that plug into them) put more audio and MIDI recording, editing, processing and mixing power at your fingertips than even their most well-equipped real-world counterparts could have hoped to match only 20 years ago. What's rather more difficult to come by, though, is the knowledge required to put all that good stuff to use – which is where this book comes in.

A comprehensive guide to Logic Pro, taking you through all the key concepts in a succinct, easy-to-understand way, *Apple Logic Pro Basics* is sure to serve as a trusty companion on your music-making journey, whether you're a total beginner or a more advanced producer looking to brush up on the basics. Work through it methodically from start to finish, or keep it by your side for reference – just don't forget to give us a credit on your debut album.

**Ronan Macdonald**
*Music technology writer and editor*

# INTRODUCTION

**Making music, recording it and sharing it has never been easier, and no software gives you more tools to enhance your songs and productions in a cool, modern way than Apple's Logic Pro. This book will get you started with this professional music-making package.**

## HEAR... AND NOW

This book uses the current incarnation of Apple Logic – Logic Pro X – to get you familiar with the Logic environment and tools. Certain references may be new to those using older versions of the software.

## SMALL CHUNKS

Every chapter has short paragraphs describing particular features within Logic Pro and how to use them. They don't have to be read in order; just dip into individual sections as needed.

**Right:** Logic Pro X is the current incarnation of Apple Logic.

## STEP-BY-STEP GUIDES

With so many features, pro-level digital-audio apps like Logic Pro can be confusing at first. This book takes many of the processes available to you and breaks them down into easy-to-follow, step-by-step instructions.

## INSIDE THE BOOK

This book is split into five sections. The first covers the basic set-up of Logic Pro with Mac OS X and how to get your project started. The second jumps into the recording process with audio and MIDI. Then we look at the extensive editing tools available for sound-shaping and signal-processing as you arrange your tracks. After that we take you through the mixing process in Logic. Finally, the last section shows you how to prepare your final mix for burning onto CD or uploading to music sites and sharing with others.

**Left:** Perhaps this book will help your musical dreams come true?

Presented to
John Appleseed

Throughout the book you will find Hot Tip boxes that give brief, handy hints and extra pieces of advice.

ALL ABOUT LOGIC PRO

# THE LOGICAL APPROACH TO MUSIC

**Logic Pro is a professional digital audio workstation (DAW) that has been an Apple product since the company acquired its original developer, Emagic, in 2002.**

**Above:** Logic Pro is known for its ease of use and an extensive library of sounds.

## WHAT CAN I DO WITH LOGIC?

The latest version of Logic, Logic Pro X, allows you to create any kind of audio production, whether you work entirely 'inside the box', using just the computer and its library of sounds, or more traditionally, using instruments like guitars, drums and keyboards, as well as microphones, with audio and MIDI (Musical Instrument Digital Interface) interfaces.

You can also create advanced productions that incorporate video, large numbers of audio tracks and extensive effects with plug-ins.

## DAWS AND BASIC RECORDING

Computer DAWs record audio signals and MIDI data generated by acoustic and electronic instruments through hardware interfaces attached to the USB or other ports on your computer. The recording process itself can be broken down into four stages.

**Above:** Logic Pro X's main screen, showing Library, Tracks and Event panes.

- ○ **Recording**: In today's world, this means the computer and its digital audio workstation software. External audio signals are digitized by the audio interface, stored on the hard drive and brought together with recorded or manually entered MIDI data (used to trigger samples and synthesizers) on the tracks that make up a multitrack project.

- ○ **Mixing**: The process of arranging the levels and character of the tracks to create the final mix of sounds. Producers have an almost limitless number of tools at their disposal.

- ○ **Mastering**: This is the final processing that gives a mix the sheen and power to compete at a high level with other recordings and ensures that all mixes in a project are uniform.

- ○ **Distribution**: The process of preparing and releasing the mastered project on media such as CDs or DVDs, or through uploads to digital music services and stores.

# INSTALLING LOGIC

After years of different versions and revisions, Logic is now simply Logic Pro X and is installed by direct download from the App Store on OS X desktops and laptops.

## YOUR MAC

To run Logic Pro X, you'll need:

- ○ 4 GB of RAM.
- ○ Display with 1280 x 768 resolution or higher.
- ○ OS X version 10.8.4 or later.

Logic requires a minimum of 5 GB of disk space and is compatible with 64-bit Audio Units' plug-ins. You'll also want at least 40 GB of free space on your internal hard drive to handle the free library content.

**Above:** You need OS X version 10.8.4 or later to run Logic Pro X.

**Above:** You need at least 40 GB of hard drive space to handle Logic's library.

Apple has a companion app called Logic Remote that lets you control many features of Logic from your iPad.

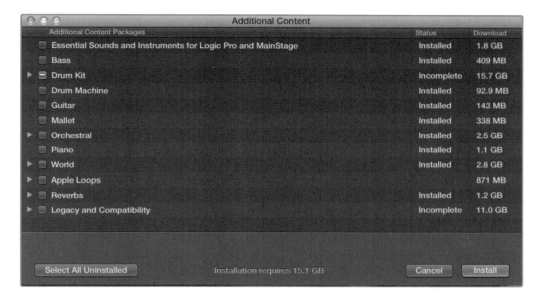

**Above:** The download screen for free Library content.

# PREPARE TO LAUNCH

After you've downloaded and installed Logic Pro X, you'll want to avail yourself of all the cool synths, sounds and loops that Apple provides before starting your first project.

# IN THE LIBRARY

The first time you open Logic Pro, it downloads basic content including software instrument presets and Apple Loops that you can use in your projects. After the download is complete, the Project Chooser opens so you can create a new project or open an existing one.

**Right:** The Library pane after downloading Logic's free additional sounds.

# YOUR NEW PROJECT

**With Logic and its library of sounds now installed, you're ready to jump in with a new or existing project.**

## FROM SCRATCH

If you want to build your project from the ground up, click New in the File menu. A screen will open with selection boxes for you to choose which kind of track you want to start with. Many people will choose Drummer (described on page 54) to get access to built-in beats and loops. Selecting Software Instrument or External MIDI will give you access to traditional drum programming and instruments, either built-in or external.

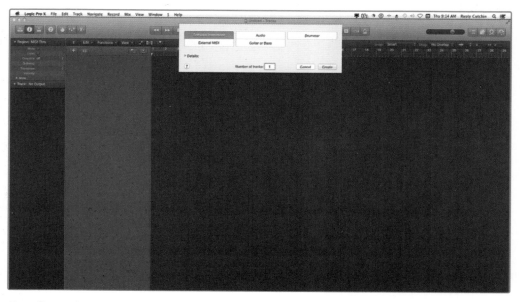

**Above:** You may choose to start an entirely new project from scratch.

## USING TEMPLATES

If you're looking for inspiration, templates are the way to go. Click New from Template in the File menu and you're presented with arrangements of tracks and instruments that you can work with, modify and save to create your own templates for future projects.

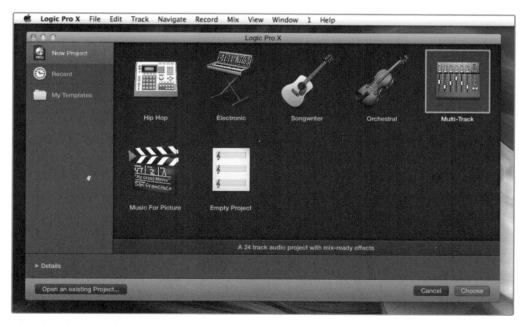

**Above:** Logic's built-in templates are a great source of inspiration.

# STANDARD TEMPLATES OVERVIEW

Logic's built-in templates are designed for songwriters and composers in all genres from pop tunesmith to film scorer. Here's what the included ones look like.

**Above:** The Hip-Hop template with String Ensemble selected in the Tracks area (centre).

## Hip-Hop

An arrangement with six tracks including a classic 808-style drum machine, synths and string ensemble. Each drum from the 808 is on its own track.

## Electronic

A 20-track set-up (16 tracks from two drum-machine groups) with various synth sounds – a good starting point for electronic dance music (EDM).

**Above:** The Hip-Hop template's Tracks area showing a grouping of drum sounds.

**Above:** The Songwriter template uses the Drummer feature and audio tracks.

## Songwriter

The Songwriter template loads a Drummer track (described on page 55) and four audio tracks set up for acoustic guitar, vocal, bass, and piano inputs.

## Orchestral

The Orchestral template sets up a score layout and loads multiple instruments. Play these samples and watch your MIDI notes translate into notes on the staff immediately.

**Above:** The Multitrack template is a good starting point for bands that are miked up and ready to record.

## Multitrack

The Multitrack template opens with 24 identical tracks and a compressor on each track. Any track can be switched to a software instrument, Drummer, or loop track with one click.

## Music for Picture

The Music for Picture template loads a mix of

**Above:** The Music for Picture template with a movie file loaded. The time counter is synchronized to the clip.

audio tracks, orchestral sounds and effects associated with film production.

## Empty Project

The Empty Project template is a blank slate with the option to open one or multiple Software Instrument, External MIDI, Drummer, Audio, Guitar, or Bass Tracks.

### Hot Tip

Many third-party companies offer additional templates. Just type 'Logic Pro X templates' into your search engine.

## OPEN FOR BUSINESS

You can of course open existing projects (File > Open). Logic remembers the most recent project you were working on and opens it upon launch, but you can change this behaviour in Preferences > General > Project Handling.

# OPENING PROJECTS FROM OTHER PLATFORMS

**If you've started a recording project with other software, such as Apple's GarageBand, or even another OS, like iOS on an iPhone or iPad, you can open or import these projects into Logic Pro X.**

## OPENING PROJECTS CREATED IN EARLIER LOGIC PRO VERSIONS

Logic Pro X can open projects created in Logic Pro 5 or later. (Projects saved in Logic Pro X are not backward compatible with earlier Logic Pro versions.) When you open a project created in an earlier version, it is converted to a Logic Pro X project. In the Save dialog, you can choose to save the converted project as a project package or project folder.

- **Project package:** Project assets (e.g. audio, video, sample files, etc) are copied to the project package, or are referenced from

**Right:** The Save As dialog showing project-folder and project-package options.

another location, depending on which asset types are selected. By default, the converted project is saved inside the existing project folder, if one exists.

○ **Project folder:** Project assets are copied to the appropriate subfolders of the project folder, or are referenced from another location. By default, any existing project folder and subfolders are used, and any additional subfolders needed for project assets are created.

**Hot Tip**

After a project is saved as a Logic Pro X project, it can no longer be opened in earlier versions of Logic Pro.

## PROJECTS CREATED IN GARAGEBAND

You can open a GarageBand project in Logic Pro just as you would open a Logic Pro project. Logic Pro X automatically creates the required number, and type, of tracks to mirror those used in the GarageBand project.

**Below:** An open GarageBand 10 project. Note the similarities to the Logic interface.

- **Tempo**: The project uses the tempo of the GarageBand project.

- **Key signature**: The initial key signature mirrors the project key of the GarageBand project.

- **Instruments**: Software instrument parts are played by GarageBand instruments in Logic Pro. GarageBand instruments are automatically installed with Logic Pro.

- **Channel strip settings**: The channel strip settings of GarageBand are imported, and you can access the individual plug-ins that are inserted into a GarageBand channel strip. For more about channel strips, go to page 94.

- **Channel strip objects**: All channel strip objects are routed to Stereo Out (default stereo output pair), and immediately play out according to the Stereo Output preference chosen in the Logic Pro > Preferences > Audio > I/O Assignments > Output pane.

- **Bus effects**: The two bus effects of GarageBand (Reverb and Echo) are also translated when opened in Logic Pro. They are replaced by the PlatinumVerb and Echo on busses 1 and 2.

**Hot Tip**

**You can't open Logic Pro projects in GarageBand, and you can't export a Logic Pro project in a format that can be read by GarageBand, except as an audio file.**

## OTHER SOFTWARE DAWS

Logic Pro X can import multitrack projects that have been exported from other DAWs as an AFF (Advanced Authoring Format) file. AAF is used by other DAW applications such as Pro Tools. You can use it to import multiple audio files, retaining their track order, time positions and volume automation.

**Above**: The option to import an AAF file from the File menu.

## Import an AAF File

1. Choose File > Import > AAF, then select a file in the dialog that appears; or

2. Locate and select the AAF file in the All Files Browser, then click Open.

## Open an AAF File

1. Choose File > Open.

2. Choose the AAF file in the Open dialog.

# ABOUT AUDIO FILES

**Logic can handle several different audio file formats. Audio files imported into a Logic Pro project can be at any supported bit depth and sample rate. In addition to audio files, Logic Pro can import MIDI and project information.**

## BIT DEPTHS AND SAMPLE RATES

Logic Pro supports bit depths of 16-, 20- and 24-bit audio, and sample rates of 44.1, 48, 88.2, 96, 176.4 and 192 kHz. Logic Pro can use the file's sample rate, or can perform real-time sample rate conversions.

# AUDIO FILE FORMATS

File formats are dictated by what the project starts with or what is imported (rather than selected by the user) in almost all cases, so to follow is a description of the main file formats you can work with in Logic Pro X and how they differ from one another:

## WAVE and AIFF Files

Wave (WAV) and Audio Interchange File Format (AIFF) audio files are similar. They can be stored at different bit depths (16- and 24-bit are supported by Logic Pro) in mono, stereo or surround, and at sample rates up to 192 kHz. Logic Pro X also supports Broadcast Wave files, which can contain timing information.

> **Hot Tip**
>
> The file extension of broadcast wave files is .wav, allowing them to be read by any application that supports the standard wave file format.

## Core Audio Format Files

Core Audio Format (CAF) files are containers that support various digital formats, including AAC and the Apple Lossless Audio Codec (ALAC). Unrestricted file sizes are possible, at high sample rates and bit depths.

## Sound Designer Files

Sound Designer I and II (SDII) audio files are similar in structure to AIFF files. Use of Sound Designer format files can make transfers between Logic Pro and Avid Pro Tools software more convenient.

## MP3, Apple Lossless and AAC Files

MP3 and AAC files contain compressed audio information. They are usually far smaller than equivalent WAV, AIFF or SDII files, but there is a loss of quality compared with those formats. Apple Lossless files are also compressed, but the compression used (ALAC) doesn't discard audio information the same way MP3 files do. The sound of the compressed audio file is identical to the original recording.

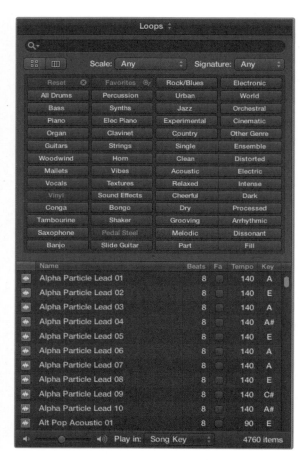

**Above:** Apple Loops in the Loop Browser.

## Apple Loops

Audio loops are audio files that contain additional information such as time and date, category, mood, key and tempo, as well as markers that divide them into small time slices. Audio loops can automatically match the tempo and key of a Logic Pro project, making them convenient for dropping into different projects with different tempos. Software instrument loops contain MIDI note information that triggers a musical phrase. When an Apple Loop is added to an audio track, the phrase is played as is; when it's added to a software instrument track, the MIDI note information can be edited.

## ReCycle Files

ReCycle (REX, RCY) files are generated in Propellerhead ReCycle software. Like Apple Loops' audio files, they contain a number of slices, and match the project tempo. Each of these slice regions can be handled like any audio region. ReCycle files, unlike Apple Loops' files, do not follow the project key.

## Standard MIDI Files

Standard MIDI Files (SMF) are data files that contain information used by sequencers to send information, including song and note data, synth patch information and other data to a MIDI device for playback or storage. You can add an SMF to MIDI or software instrument tracks in Logic Pro.

# THE PROJECT AUDIO BROWSER

This shows all audio files and regions that have been added to or recorded in your project, whether or not they are used in the Tracks area. Regions shown in the Project Audio Browser that are not used in the Tracks area are indicated in red. You can add, edit, delete and rename audio files and regions in the Project Audio Browser. You can add audio files by dragging them from the Project Audio Browser into the Tracks area, where you can edit, move and copy them. You can also open a separate Project Audio window. The Project Audio Browser is only available when Show Advanced Tools is selected in the Advanced Preferences pane.

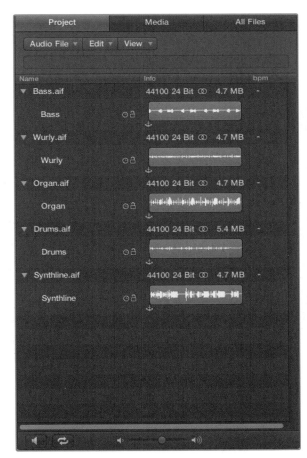

## Open the Project Audio Browser

You can open the Project Audio Browser in two ways:

1. Click the Browsers button in the control bar, then click Project.

2. Choose View > Show Browsers (or press B), then click Project.

## Open a Separate Project Audio Window

Choose Window > Open Project Audio (or press Command+9).

**Above:** Project Audio Browser.

# INTEGRATING YOUR iPHONE OR iPAD

There are many ways to use external hardware with your desktop or laptop Mac and Logic Pro X. In the past few years, several novel ways to use your iOS devices with Logic have emerged. You'll need some extras, though, to enhance your capabilities.

## HARDWARE FOR iPAD AND iPHONE

Unless you just want to work with downloaded loops and sounds, you'll need an audio interface (see page 32). Some, such as the Apogee One, are specifically designed to work with an iPad and iPhone.

## SOFTWARE OPTIONS

Logic Control is currently the only app that lets you control Logic Pro remotely from an iPad.

**Above:** The Apogee One is a high-quality audio interface MFi (Made For iPad).

**Above:** Logic Pro X on a MacBook Pro with Logic Remote on an iPad.

Other audio apps, such as Cubasis and Auria, let you record tracks for later transfer to Logic.

## FILE MANAGEMENT

When you've created your tracks on your iPad, you can either upload the audio files to a cloud-based storage service (such as Dropbox), or use a utility like Ecamm Network's PhoneView on your Mac. Use Logic's Import control, and you're ready to add the tracks to a new or existing project.

Logic Control is great for drummers recording to a Mac situated in a different room to the one they're playing in.

**Below**: PhoneView can retrieve audio (or other) files from your iPad or iPhone to use with Logic.

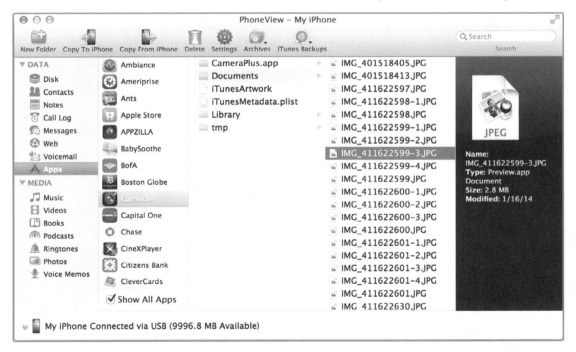

RECORDING WITH LOGIC PRO

# CONNECTING EXTERNAL HARDWARE

Now that you've got a Logic Pro X project open, you can make music with its internal tools, like Apple Loops and Drummer; but to create your own musical parts you'll need essential hardware like an audio interface and MIDI keyboard.

## THE AUDIO INTERFACE

Audio interfaces range from small tabletop boxes to large-format mixers. They're used to digitize the audio signals you create with microphones or electric instruments; and many also enable the connection of MIDI instruments, like MIDI keyboards and drum machines.

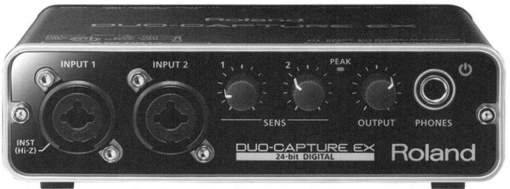

**Above:** The compact Roland Duo-Capture EX USB audio interface.

### Understanding MIDI Recording

The Musical Instrument Digital Interface (MIDI) was incorporated into synthesizers in the 1980s before personal computers were around. The acronym describes not only the connectors on your keyboard or audio interface but also the data that's generated whenever you strike a key, rotate a pitch wheel, step on a sustain pedal or carry out any of several other actions on a MIDI instrument.

## Understanding Audio Recording

Today's higher-quality mics and analog-to-digital converters capture audio signals better than ever before. A modern audio interface may incorporate only one microphone connector or many more on mixers/interfaces. After incoming signals are digitized, they are stored in the computer as audio files that can be placed on tracks in Logic Pro X or any other DAW.

**Above:** The Mackie Onyx 1640i mixer with FireWire audio interface.

# MAKING THE CONNECTION

To fully equip your recording set-up, you'll need to connect external mics and instruments to the audio/MIDI interface and connect the interface to the computer.

## Connect the Interface to the Computer

Many interfaces designed to

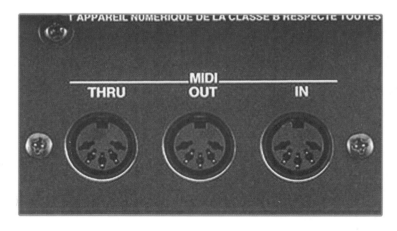

**Above:** A MIDI keyboard's rear panel, showing MIDI In, Out and Thru ports.

work with Macs make use of Firewire 400 or 800 ports. Higher-end interfaces make use of the Mac's Thunderbolt ports.

**Above:** Audio interface showing Mic and Instrument inputs and controls.

## Connect MIDI Instruments to the Interface

Connect your external keyboards to the MIDI In and MIDI Out ports on the audio interface or a separate USB MIDI interface. Lower-end keyboard controllers, which generate MIDI data but don't generate sound, can connect directly to the USB ports.

## Connect Audio Outputs

The audio interface will supply the various sounds you're creating to your speaker system for monitoring while you're recording and to hear playback. The speakers may be part of a system as simple as a home stereo or as complex as a professional recording console with multiple power amps.

## Connect Instrument Inputs

If you plan to record sounds from external instruments like electric guitars, synths, drum machines, or other electric/electronic sound-generating devices, connect

*Hot Tip*

**Always match the output of your instrument to the correct input on the interface.**

those to the audio inputs of the interface. If the interface is built into a mixer, you'll have lots of available inputs for your audio devices. Smaller interfaces will have fewer options.

## Connect Microphones

For your vocals and acoustic instruments, you may need a range of microphones. Studio-quality microphones use XLR cables with three-pin connectors, while mixers/interfaces will have multiple inputs to accommodate recording bands, which will require several mics to handle drums and acoustic instruments. Some electric instruments like bass guitar use a converter, called a direct box, to create a mic-level signal for its more pristine character.

### Hot Tip

Dynamic mics can be connected to any mic input, but condenser mics require a channel with 48-volt phantom power.

**Above:** Rear of audio interface showing MIDI, USB and monitor connections.

# LOGIC PRO PROJECTS

A project is a Logic Pro document that contains all of your recordings, the location of media files, and all your edits. Each project has properties that include tempo, key and time signature, and more. A project can also include assets, such as audio and video files, sampler instruments, samples and reverb files.

## MAIN WINDOW AND TRACKS AREA

The Logic Pro main window is where you work on your projects, from which you can access all of the major working areas of Logic Pro.

Control Bar          **Below:** Logic Pro X main window with main working areas.          Tracks area

Inspector          Tracks area

## Tracks Area

The central part of the window is the Tracks area, where you record and arrange the musical material in your project. There are several different track types, including audio, software instrument and Drummer tracks.

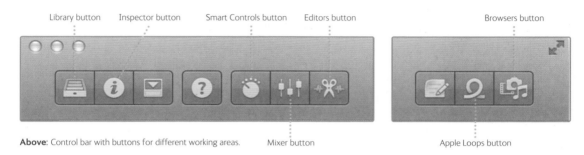

Library button     Inspector button     Smart Controls button     Editors button     Browsers button

Mixer button     Apple Loops button

**Above**: Control bar with buttons for different working areas.

## Control Bar

Situated at the top of the main window, the control bar includes buttons that let you access different parts of Logic Pro, transport controls for controlling playback, a Master Volume slider, and others. In the centre of the control bar is the LCD, where you can view the current playhead position, move the playhead, and set the project tempo, key and time signature.

## Library

You can audition patches and choose a patch for the selected track in the Library. A patch contains the instrument, effects and routing settings that control the sound of a track. In addition to patches, you can view and select plug-in presets and other settings in the Library.

**Left**: The Library with the Piano category and a Grand Piano patch selected.

**Above:** The inspector, showing the Quick Help area, the Region inspector, Track inspector and Inspector channel strips.

## Inspector

You can view and edit parameters for the selected region, track and other items in the Inspector. The available inspectors and parameters change, depending on which working area you are in, and what is selected.

**Above:** The Smart Controls pane showing a set of Electric Piano screen controls.

## Smart Controls

Smart Controls let you quickly adjust the sound of the selected track. When you open the Smart Controls pane, you see the onscreen controls for the selected track.

## Mixer

The Mixer is where you adjust volume, pan and other channel strip settings, mute and solo channel strips, add and edit plug-ins assigned to a channel strip, and control the signal flow of your project.

**Above:** The Mixer showing audio, software instrument, auxiliary, output and master channel strips.

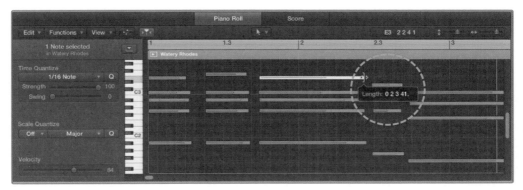

**Above:** Editing a MIDI note event in the Piano Roll Editor.

**Above:** The Loop Browser showing keyword buttons and matching loops in the Results list.

## Editors

Logic Pro includes a set of Editors, which you can use to edit individual tracks and regions, and manipulate their contents precisely. The available Editors depends on the type of track or region selected.

## Loop Browser

Logic Pro includes an extensive collection of prerecorded Apple Loops that you can add to your projects. You browse or search for loops in the Loop Browser, where you can also preview them.

## Media Browser

Browse your computer and connected storage devices for audio files and movies. When Show Advanced Tools is selected in the Advanced Preferences pane, additional features, browsers, and editors are available.

**Above:** The All Files Browser showing the Audio Files and Bounces folders, and audio files in the Logic folder.

# PLAYBACK AND NAVIGATION

**You can play back the project at any time to hear your latest changes. You control playback and navigate the project using the playhead, the ruler and the transport buttons, located in the control bar.**

**Above:** The top of the Tracks area showing the ruler and the playhead.

## START AND STOP PLAYBACK

To start playback, click the Play button (or press the Space-bar). When the project is playing, the Go to Beginning button becomes a Stop button. To stop playback, click the Stop button

Rewind button          Play button

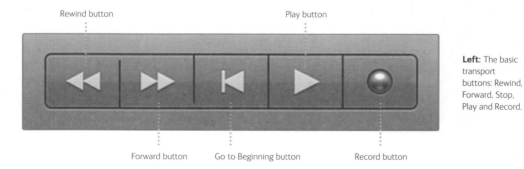

**Left:** The basic transport buttons: Rewind, Forward, Stop, Play and Record.

Forward button     Go to Beginning button     Record button

(or press the Space-bar again). To start playback from the clicked position, double-click the lower part of the ruler. Double-click again to stop playback.

## MOVE THE PLAYHEAD

Drag the playhead to a new position, or click the lower part of the ruler to move the playhead to the clicked position. If the project is playing, playback continues from the clicked position. While the project is playing, click the Rewind or Forward button. Each time you click Rewind, the playhead jumps back to the previous bar. Each time you click Forward, the playhead jumps forward to the next bar. In the LCD, click-hold one of the numbers in the Position display and drag vertically.

You can use the cycle area to define a section of the timeline to play back repeatedly. When you turn on the cycle area, it appears as a yellow strip in the upper part of the ruler.

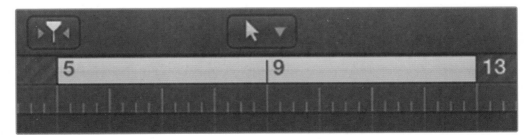

**Above:** The cycle area in the upper part of the ruler.

# THE PROJECT TEMPO, KEY AND TIME SIGNATURES

Each project has a set of properties, including tempo, key signature and time signature, which are displayed in the LCD in the control bar. You can change these properties when you create a project, or later while you're working.

## TEMPO

The tempo defines the musical speed of the project, expressed as the number of beats per minute (bpm). To set the tempo in the LCD, click-hold the tempo value (above the letters 'bpm') and drag up or down.

### Hot Tip

For new projects, the default project tempo is 120 bpm, the key is C and the time signature is 4/4.

**Above:** Editing the tempo in the LCD.

## KEY

The project key defines the central note (called the tonic) and whether the project uses the major or minor scale. To set the project key in the LCD, click-hold the key, then choose a new key from the pop-up menu.

# TIME SIGNATURE

The time signature contains two numbers separated by a slash (/). The first number controls the number of beats in each bar (or measure) and the second number controls the note value of each beat. To set the project time signature in the LCD, click-hold either of the numbers above the word 'signature', then drag up or down.

# SHOW PROJECT PROPERTIES IN THE LCD

Click the icon on the left side of the LCD, then choose Beats & Project from the pop-up menu. When Show Advanced Tools is selected in the Advanced Preferences pane, you can add tempo, key and time signature changes in a project.

**Above:** Selecting Beats & Project in the LCD to display project properties.

# GET STARTED WITH AUDIO TRACKS

**You can record sound from a microphone or from an electric instrument connected to your computer on an audio track in the Tracks area. The recording appears as an audio region on the selected audio track, showing an audio waveform.**

## PATCHES

When you add a track, you can choose a patch for the track from the Library. Each audio patch contains one or more audio effects, and can include sends and other routing settings. In the Library, click a category on the left. Click a patch name on the right. You can audition audio patches by clicking them, then playing your instrument, singing or making sound.

**Above:** Audio tracks and audio regions in the Tracks area.

## ADD AN AUDIO TRACK

1. Click the Add Tracks button in the toolbar.

2. Click one of the two Audio icons at the top of the New Tracks dialog.

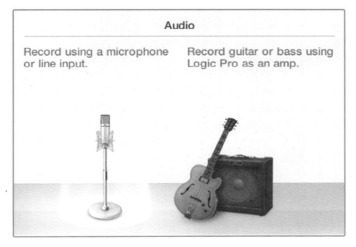

Audio

Record using a microphone or line input.

Record guitar or bass using Logic Pro as an amp.

**Above:** Selecting an Audio icon in the New Tracks dialog.

3. To create an audio track for recording from a microphone, click the microphone icon.

4. To create an audio track for recording a guitar or bass connected to your computer, click the guitar icon.

5. If necessary, click the Details triangle to open the bottom of the dialog.

6. Choose the audio device and input channel (or stereo pair) from the Input pop-up menu on the left.

7. Make sure that 'Output 1-2' appears on the Output pop-up menu.

8. Click Create.

# PREPARE FOR AUDIO RECORDING

1.  Make sure that your microphone or instrument is connected to the audio input on your computer or your audio interface, and is working.

2.  Make sure there is enough free storage space on your computer's hard drive or connected storage device.

3.  Sing or play, and check the input level meter in the track header to be sure that the track is receiving the audio signal.

4.  To hear the sound from your microphone or instrument while you're recording, click the Input Monitoring button in the track header.

Input Monitoring button

**Above:** Audio track header, showing the Input Monitoring button selected.

## RECORD ON AN AUDIO TRACK

1. Select the header of the audio track you want to record on.

2. Move the playhead to the point where you want to start recording.

3. Click the Record button in the control bar (or press R) to start recording.

4. Start singing or play your instrument.

**Above:** An audio track in the Tracks area showing a new audio region being recorded.

5. After a one-bar count-in, recording starts. The recording appears as a new audio region on the track as you record.

6. Click the Stop button in the control bar (or press the Space-bar) to stop recording.

You can record multiple takes simultaneously, and quickly create comps (composite takes) of the best moments from each take.

**Above:** The Tracks area showing the new audio region after recording.

# SOFTWARE INSTRUMENT TRACKS

**If you have a USB or MIDI keyboard connected to your computer, you can play and record software instruments.**

## INSTRUMENT LIBRARY

Logic Pro features a complete library of pro-quality software instruments. Your recording appears as a MIDI region on the selected software instrument track. You can arrange MIDI regions in the Tracks area, and edit them in the Piano Roll Editor and other editors.

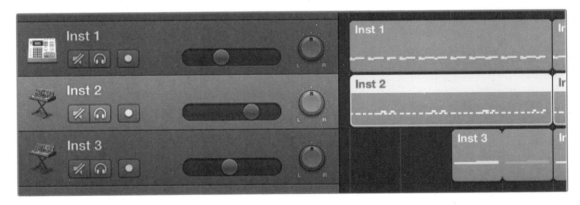

**Above:** The Tracks area showing software instrument regions on software instrument tracks.

## PLAY A SOFTWARE INSTRUMENT

To play a software instrument, first select a software instrument track, then play notes on your music keyboard. If your music keyboard has pitch bend and modulation wheels, move them as you play, to see how the sound changes. If your music keyboard has other controls, such as faders, knobs or drum pads, try using them as well.

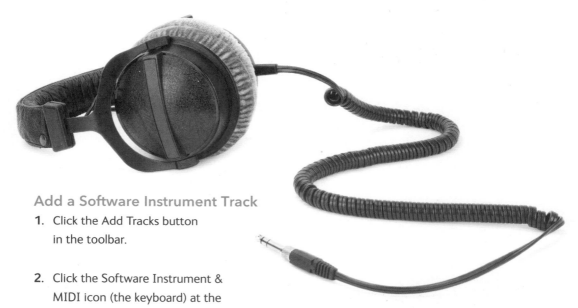

### Add a Software Instrument Track

1. Click the Add Tracks button
   in the toolbar.

2. Click the Software Instrument &
   MIDI icon (the keyboard) at the
   top of the New Tracks dialog.

3. If necessary, click the Details triangle
   to open the bottom of the dialog.

4. Make sure that 'A Software Instrument'
   appears on the pop-up menu on the left,
   and 'Output 1-2' appears on the Output
   pop-up menu on the right.

5. Make sure the Open Library checkbox
   is selected.

6. Click Create. The new track appears in
   the Tracks area and the Library opens on
   the left.

**Below:** Selecting the Software
Instrument & MIDI button in the New Tracks dialog.

**Instrument & MIDI**

Play sounds from your Mac or
external MIDI device, or connect
other apps to Logic Pro.

### Choose a Software Instrument Patch

In the Library, click a category on the left, then click a patch name on the right. You can audition software instrument patches by clicking them in the Library, then playing your music keyboard.

## RECORD A SOFTWARE INSTRUMENT

1. Select the software instrument track you want to record to.

2. Move the playhead to the point where you want to start recording.

3. Click the Record button in the control bar (or press R) to start recording.

4. After a one-bar count-in, recording starts. The recording appears as a new software instrument region on the track as you record.

5. Click the Stop button in the control bar (or press the Space-bar) to stop recording.

# TRACK HEADER CONTROLS

Each track has a header that shows the name and icon, and features a number of controls including Mute, Solo and Record Enable. Audio tracks also feature an Input Monitoring button.

## LIST OF CONTROLS IN THE TRACK HEADER

The track headers are located along the left side of the Tracks area, so you can easily see the settings for all tracks while working.

Mute button                                          Volume button

Solo button                                          Pan/Balance knob

### Mute a Track

Click the track's Mute button in the track header.

**Above:** Track headers, showing the Mute and Solo buttons, Volume slider and Pan/Balance knob.

### Solo a Track

Click the track's Solo button in the track header. The Solo button turns yellow, and the Mute buttons of all unsoloed tracks flash blue. Click the button a second time to restore the track to its previous state.

## Adjust a Track's Volume Level

In the track header, drag the Volume slider left to lower the volume level, or drag it right to raise the volume level. Option-click the slider to return it to a neutral level (0 dB gain).

## Adjust a Track's Pan or Balance Position

In the track header, drag the Pan/Balance knob counterclockwise to pan to the left, or drag clockwise to pan to the right. The dot on the wheel indicates the pan position. Option-click the Pan/Balance knob to return it to the centre position.

## Change Track Buttons on Multiple Tracks

Click-hold a button on a track header, then drag the pointer up or down over additional tracks. The corresponding buttons on all the swiped tracks will switch to the same state.

# DRUMMER OVERVIEW

You can add a virtual drummer to your project, using a Drummer track. You can only have one Drummer track per project.

## DRUMMER OPTIONS

You can choose drummers from different genres – Alternative, Rock, Songwriter and R&B. Each Drummer comes with its own drum kit and a distinct playing style. You can change the drummer's playing style in the Drummer Editor by choosing different presets, tweaking the generated pattern using various settings, or by having Drummer regions follow the rhythm of another track in the project.

**Hot Tip**

To edit Drummer regions in the Piano Roll Editor, Event List, or Step Editor, first convert them to MIDI regions.

You can influence the sound of the drums further by choosing patches in the Library or by exchanging drums and editing the settings of individual kit pieces in Drum Kit Designer.

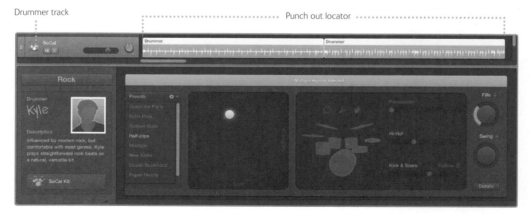

**Above:** A Drummer track containing Drummer regions and the Drummer Editor.

## Default Patch

When you add a Drummer track to your project, a drummer and a default patch are loaded. The default patch is based on a stereo mixdown of the full, multi-miked drum kit mix.

# ADD A DRUMMER TRACK

1. Choose Track > New Drummer Track.

2. In the New Tracks dialog, select the Drummer track. Click Create.

3. If the project does not have arrangement markers, a Drummer track containing two 8-bar regions is created. Two different presets associated with the drummer are loaded to the two regions.

**Above:** A Drummer track containing two 8-bar regions.

4. If the project has arrangement markers, a Drummer track containing as many regions as there are arrangement markers is created. The length and name of the Drummer regions correspond to the existing arrangement markers.

**Above:** A Drummer track containing five regions to match the five arrangement markers.

# RECORD YOUR VOICE OR A MUSICAL INSTRUMENT

**In Logic Pro, you can use different methods when recording voices, acoustic instruments and software instruments, including take recording, multitrack recording and replace recording.**

## BEFORE RECORDING AUDIO

Go through the following checklist carefully before embarking on your recording.

1. Check hardware connections and settings, ensuring any sound source you plan to use – e.g. microphone or mixer – is connected to the audio inputs of your system and is working. Check you have enough disk space.

2. Add an audio track, which is used to record a voice, an acoustic instrument, or any other sound from a microphone.

3. Choose the recording file type – AIFF, WAV or CAF – before recording (see page 22 for more information on file types).

4. Set the audio recording path (only necessary if you want to save recorded audio outside of the project).

5. Set the project sample rate (the number of times per second

### Hot Tip

If Fade Out is turned on, it will be temporarily disabled while recording, so that you can hear what you record.

the audio signal is sampled). A sample rate of 44.1 kHz is recommended for most situations.

6. Set the project bit depth, which is the number of digital bits each sample contains. A bit depth of 24 bits is the default setting.

7. Set up the metronome, which plays a steady beat so you can play and record in time or as a count-in before recording starts.

8. Enable software monitoring, which allows you to monitor incoming audio through any effects that are inserted into an armed audio track.

9. Check the monitoring level, which controls the playback (or monitoring) level, not the recording level.

**Right**: When you're ready to record audio, the New Tracks dialog gives you the choice of recording from a mic or a guitar.

# RECORD SOUND FROM A MICROPHONE OR AN ELECTRIC INSTRUMENT

You can record sound from a microphone (e.g. voice or acoustic instrument), or from an electric instrument (e.g. electric guitar) on an audio track.

## Record Live Audio

1. Select the header of the audio or guitar/bass track you want to record to.

2. Move the playhead to the point in the ruler where you want to start recording.

3. Logic Pro includes a metronome, which plays a steady beat to help you play in time while recording. Turn this on or off using the Metronome button in the control bar.

> **Hot Tip**
>
> For the initial setup, choose Record > Count-in, then choose a measure.

**Below:** Selecting the header of an audio track.

**4.** Click the Count-in button to have the metronome play a predefined count-in before recording starts.

**5.** Click the Record button in the control bar (or press R) to start recording.

**6.** Start singing or play your instrument. The recording appears as a new audio region on the track as you record.

**Above:** Showing a recorded audio region in red in the Tracks area.

**7.** Click the Stop button in the control bar (or press the Space-bar) to stop recording.

When Show Advanced Tools is selected in the Advanced Preferences pane, you can view the newly recorded audio region in the Project Audio Browser.

# PUNCH RECORDING

Punch recording is a technique used to overwrite a portion of a previously recorded track, during playback, without affecting any of the recording before or after that portion. You can choose between two punch-recording modes – Quick Punch-In and Autopunch.

Punch-in locator                                        Punch-out locator

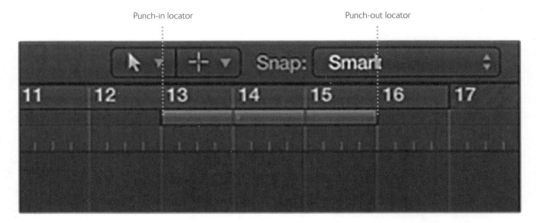

**Above:** The Autopunch area is indicated by a red stripe in the middle of the ruler. The left and right autopunch locators indicate the punch-in and punch-out points.

## QUICK PUNCH-IN MODE

This mode helps you fix mistakes or create alternate takes for a particular section. When Quick Punch-In mode is on, recording occurs in the background from the moment you start playback. This means that there needs to be twice as many available channel strips as the number enabled for recording. A dialog appears if you exceed the number of channels needed.

*Hot Tip*

Punch recording is only available when Show Advanced Tools is selected in the Advanced Preferences pane.

# AUTOPUNCH MODE

Autopunch lets you set punch-in and punch-out points at which to start and stop recording so you can concentrate on your playing, rather than on controlling the software. You can also set the starting and stopping of recordings more precisely than in Quick Punch-In mode.

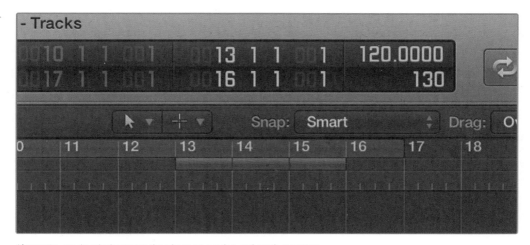

**Above:** You can drag the locators in the ruler to set punch-in and punch-out points.

# USE STEP INPUT RECORDING TECHNIQUES

Step Input allows you to insert MIDI notes when you're not in a real-time recording mode. You can use Step Input to create note runs that may be too fast for you to play, or to replicate sheet music that's too difficult for you to play. You can use one or more of the following for Step Input:

1. Musical typing keyboard.
2. Step Input keyboard.
3. MIDI keyboard.

The Step Input keyboard is only available when Show Advanced Tools is selected in the Advanced Preferences pane.

# ARRANGING & EDITING WITH LOGIC PRO

# MODIFYING RECORDED TRACKS

**Logic Pro X lets you arrange and rearrange music to your heart's content before committing to a mix. In this section we'll get you started with Logic's many tools for arranging and editing recorded audio.**

## ARRANGING OVERVIEW

After adding audio, MIDI and Drummer regions to your project, you build the project by arranging the regions in the Tracks area. As you work in the Tracks area, you can play the project at any time to hear your latest changes and you can do any of the following:

1. Arrange regions in a variety of ways.

2. Create and edit fades, and create automatic crossfades on audio regions.

3.  Remove silent passages from audio files.

4.  Use folders to manage groups of tracks as a single unit.

5.  Use groove templates to apply the rhythmic feel of a region to other audio or MIDI regions.

6.  Edit region parameters to control the sound of both audio and MIDI regions.

**Below**: You can arrange regions in the Tracks window in a variety of ways.

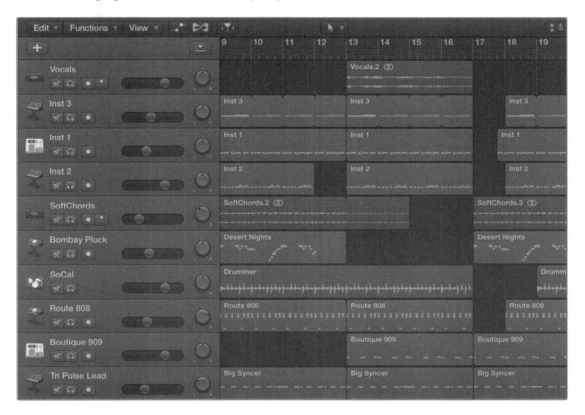

# TRACKS AREA OVERVIEW

The Tracks area, located in the centre of the Logic Pro main window, shows a visual representation of time moving from left to right. Here you build your project by arranging regions in rows, called tracks, that run from the beginning to the end of the Tracks area.

The playhead extends from the top to the bottom of the Tracks area, and moves as the project plays. At the top of the playhead is a triangle that you can drag to move the playhead to a different part of the project, or scrub the regions in the Tracks area. You can also scroll to see another part of the project and zoom in for precise editing or zoom out to see more of the project.

**Above:** Tracks area showing tracks and regions, the playhead and the ruler.

# REGIONS IN THE TRACKS AREA

Regions are the building blocks of a project, representing your recordings, Apple Loops and other media files you add to the project. Regions appear as rounded rectangles in the Tracks area. There are several different types of regions, depending on the track type. The two primary region types are audio regions, which show the audio waveform, and MIDI regions, which show note events as thin rectangles.

**Above:** The Tracks area showing audio, software instrument and Drummer regions.

# ARRANGING REGIONS

You can arrange regions in a variety of ways in the Tracks area, by moving, looping, resizing, splitting, joining and deleting them. Try following the tasks below, using regions in the project.

## Move a Region

To move a region, do any of the following:

1. Drag a region left or right to move it to a new time position.

2. Drag an audio region up or down to another audio track.

3. Drag a MIDI region up or down to another software instrument track.

## Resize a Region

1. Move the pointer over the lower-right edge of the region and it becomes a Resize pointer.

2. Drag the edge of the region horizontally to shorten or lengthen it.

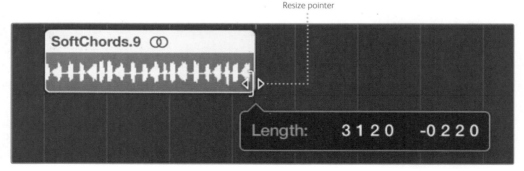

**Above**: Resizing a region in the Tracks area. The Help tag shows the length of the region.

## Loop a Region

1. Place the pointer over the upper-right edge of the region and it becomes a Loop pointer.

2. Drag the right edge of the region several bars to the right.

3. When you drag the edge of the region out by its full length, rounded corners indicate the beginning and end of each complete repetition of the region.

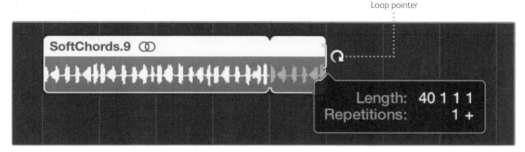

**Above:** Looping a region in the Tracks area. The Help tag shows the region length and the number of repetitions.

## Split a Region Using the Playhead

1. Select the region you want to split.

2. Move the playhead over the point in the region where you want to split it, then choose Edit > Split.

Only the selected region is split, even if an unselected region on another track is under the playhead as well. If multiple regions are selected and are under the playhead, they are all split.

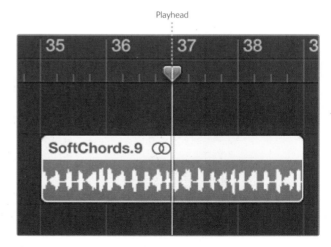

**Above:** Splitting a region in the Tracks area using the playhead.

## Split a Region Using the Scissors Tool

1. Select the region you want to split.

2. Select the Scissors Tool, then click-hold the region.

3. The Help tag shows the current split position.

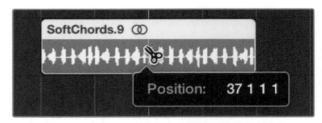

SoftChords.9

Position:   37 1 1 1

4. Release the mouse button.

**Above:** Splitting a region in the Tracks area using the Scissors Tool.

When selecting a cut point with the Scissors Tool, you can move backward and forward in steps of one division. The grid is based on the Snap pop-up menu setting.

## Delete a Region

Select the region, then choose Edit > Delete (or press the Delete key).

# CREATE FADES

Fades are only visible if you are zoomed in enough to see the waveform in the audio region. You can create a fade using either the Fade tool or the Fade In and Fade Out parameters in the Region inspector.

## Using The Fade Tool

1. Select the Fade tool.

Fade Tool

**Left:** The Fade tool.

2. Choose one:

    1. Drag over the start or end point of an audio region. A fade-in or fade-out is created. The length of the fade drag area determines the length of the fade (longer drag area = longer fade time, a shorter drag area = a quick fade).

    2. Drag over the end point of one audio region and the start point of the region that follows.

This technique works even if the two sections aren't directly joined. With the Fade tool selected, you can edit fades on regions after you make them.

**Above:** A pair of images showing fade-in creation on a region using the Fade tool.

**Below:** A pair of images showing fade creation between regions using the Fade tool.

## Using the Region Inspector

**1.** Select one or more regions.

**2.** Set the value for the Fade In or Fade Out setting in the Region inspector by dragging the pointer vertically, or double-clicking and entering a value.

Fades created using the Fade tool and the Region inspector are interactive. After you create a fade using the Fade tool, for example, you can adjust the fade using the Region inspector Fade In or Fade Out parameters.

**Below**: Fade In parameter in the Region inspector, also reflected in the Arrange area.

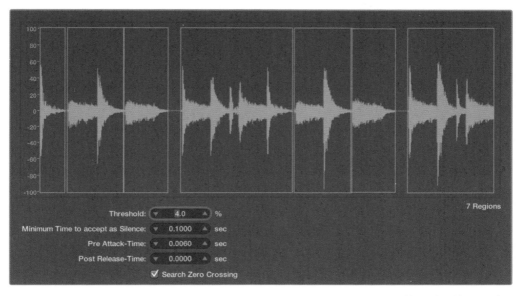

**Above:** Strip Silence window.

# REMOVE SILENT PASSAGES
# IN THE STRIP SILENCE WINDOW

The basic process is simple: all amplitude values below a threshold level are removed, and new regions are created from the remaining passages. You can use Strip Silence for a variety of different situations.

- Remove background noises.
- Create segments of spoken recordings.
- Create segments for drum loops.
- Optimize files and regions.
- Extract audio files from discs.

To open the Strip Silence window, control-click an audio region in the Project Audio Browser, then choose Strip Silence from the shortcut menu.

*Hot Tip*

**All parameters can affect the number and division of regions. Try different values to see what produces the best result.**

### Remove Silent Passages from a Selected Region

1. Set parameters in the Strip Silence window.

2. Click OK. If you selected a region that is used in the Tracks area, a dialog asks if you want to replace the region in the Tracks area.

3. Choose one:
    1. To replace the region in the Tracks area with regions created by the Strip Silence function, click Replace or press Return. This ensures that the relative timing of the individual audio segments remains unaltered.

    2. To have the regions appear only in the Project Audio Browser, click No. You can add regions manually from the Project Audio Browser.

## GROOVE TEMPLATES

You can create quantization grids – groove templates – based on the rhythms of audio or MIDI regions. Groove templates can be used to capture the subtle timing deviations that give a region its 'feel', and apply that feel to other audio or MIDI regions. You can even take the feel of an audio region and apply it to a MIDI region – helping a MIDI clarinet part to sit well with a funk guitar Apple Loop, for example.

**Below:** Audio region selected in the Tracks area.

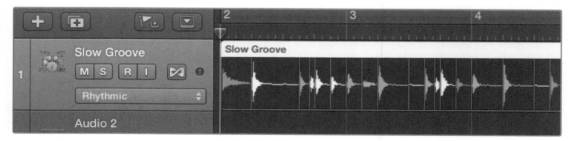

You can also select multiple regions to create a groove template, and all of them will contribute their transients or notes to the new groove template. The source audio or MIDI region used for a groove template must remain in your project if you want to use the groove template. If you delete the source region from the project, the groove template can no longer be used.

**Hot Tip**

Two-bar MIDI regions work well for groove templates, but you can use MIDI regions of any length. Make sure the source MIDI region contains a note at every desired quantization value.

## Create a Groove Template

1. Select the region(s) from which you want to create a groove template.

2. In the Region inspector, choose a quantization value from the Quantize pop-up menu.

3. Open the Quantize pop-up menu again and choose Make Groove Template (or use the corresponding key command).

4. The groove template, with the default name of the selected region, appears near the bottom of the Quantize pop-up menu, and the Quantize parameter of the parent region is set to it.

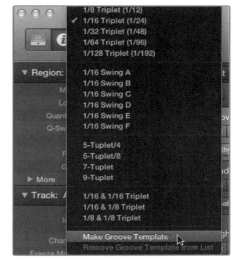

**Above:** Make Groove Template selected in the Quantize pop-up menu.

**Above:** The default groove template name selected in the Quantize pop-up menu.

# THE LOGIC PRO X EDITORS

Logic offers total control over your MIDI and audio data using various windows and tools. Here's a summary of the editing windows and how to get around them.

## AUDIO TRACK EDITOR

The Audio Track Editor displays the audio waveform of the regions on an audio track. In the Audio Track Editor, you can copy, paste, move, trim, split and join audio regions. Using the Audio Track Editor grid, you can precisely align edits with specific points in time.

- **Audio Track Editor menu bar**: Contains menus with region-editing commands and functions, as well as buttons for Flex editing, selecting editing tools and zooming the editor.

- **Audio Track Editor inspector**: When Flex Pitch is turned on, this contains controls for quantizing time and pitch, correcting pitch and adjusting gain.

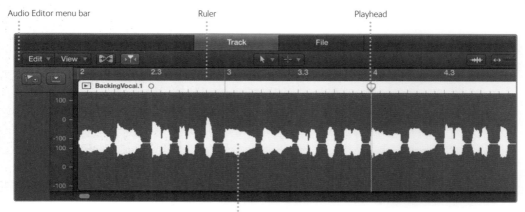

**Above:** The Audio Track Editor.

- **Waveform display**: Shows the audio waveform for the region on a time grid.

- **Ruler**: Shows time divisions so you can align regions and make edits at precise time positions.

- **Playhead**: Reflects the current playback position.

## PIANO ROLL EDITOR

The Piano Roll Editor shows notes in MIDI regions as rectangles on a time grid. The position of each note on the grid shows the time position where it starts playing, its duration (length) and pitch. Note velocity is indicated by colour. You can edit individual notes by moving them, resizing them, dragging them vertically to change their pitch, and in a variety of other ways.

- **Piano Roll Editor menu bar**: Contains menus with region-editing commands and functions, as well as buttons for selecting editing tools and zooming the Editor.

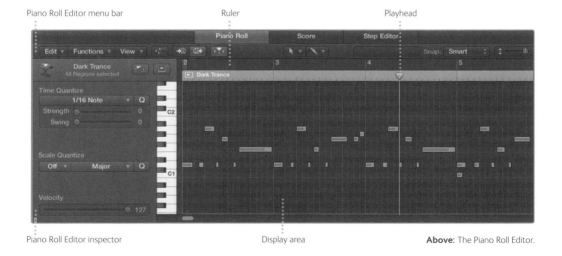

Piano Roll Editor menu bar       Ruler       Playhead

Piano Roll Editor inspector       Display area       **Above:** The Piano Roll Editor.

- **Piano Roll Editor inspector**: Contains controls for quantizing note timing and adjusting note pitch and velocity.

- **Display area**: Shows the notes in the MIDI region or regions as bars on a time grid.

- **Ruler**: Shows time divisions so you can align and edit notes at precise time positions.

- **Playhead**: Reflects the current playback position.

# DRUMMER EDITOR

If you add a Drummer track to a project, you can view and edit the Drummer track and region parameters in the Drummer Editor. The left side of the Drummer Editor shows the settings, including genres and drummers. On the right side are parameters for the selected Drummer region, including presets, an XY pad for adjusting the complexity and loudness of the region performance, and controls for editing performance parameters, including kit piece pattern variations and fill settings.

- **Genres and drummers**: Select a genre to view the drummers for that genre, then select the drummer for the track.

- **Drummer presets**: Choose a preset for the selected Drummer region. (A preset consists of all region settings, visible to the right of the presets area.) You can use the default settings, or you can edit them and save your own presets.

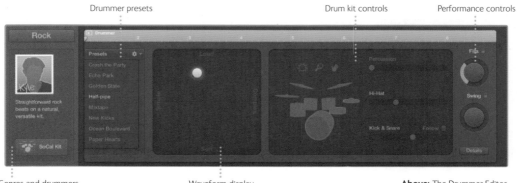

Genres and drummers          Waveform display              **Above:** The Drummer Editor.

- **XY pad**: Adjust the complexity and loudness of the region performance.

- **Drum kit controls**: Turn on different instruments, and choose between different variations for the drum and percussion pieces. You also have the option to play half time or double time for kick and snare.

- **Performance controls**: Adjust the number and length of fills using the Fills knob. Adjust the shuffle feel of the region performance using the Swing knob. Click the Details button to reveal additional performance controls.

# SCORE EDITOR

The Score Editor displays MIDI regions as music notation, including notes, rests and other MIDI events such as sustain pedal markings. You can add and edit notes and other musical

Event inspector    Region inspector                                    **Below:** The Score Editor.

Part box                                              Score working area

symbols. Lyrics, titles and other text can also be included in the score. You can control the display of individual staffs, extract parts from the score, modify the overall score layout, and print or export complete scores, partial scores and parts.

- **Score working area**: Displays music notation for selected MIDI regions, tracks, or the entire project.

- **Region inspector**: Choose visual quantization and other display settings for selected regions.

- **Event inspector**: Control appearance and position settings for individual notes and other items in the score.

- **Part box**: Displays available musical symbols, organized in groups. Select musical symbols to add to the score, and customize the order of symbols in the Part box.

# STEP EDITOR

The Step Editor displays notes or controller events for selected MIDI regions as beams in a user-defined time grid. You can easily add or edit note velocities or other controller data (making some editing tasks, such as data scaling, much faster) or quickly create and edit MIDI drum parts.

- **Lane parameters**: Determine the type of event displayed or modified. When you select a row in the name column, its event definition is shown in the Lane inspector.

- **MIDI events**: Represented by vertical beams in a time grid. Controller values, note velocity and other values are indicated by the height of each beam (taller beams indicate higher values).

Region inspector

**Below:** Hyper Editor.

Score working area

# AUDIO FILE EDITOR

The Audio File Editor is only available when Additional Options for both Audio and Advanced editing are selected in the Advanced Preferences pane. It displays the audio waveform of regions on an audio track. In the Audio File Editor, you can destructively edit audio files (and regions) and use audio processing tools to quantize audio, change sample rates and extract MIDI grooves from audio files. The Audio File Editor has its own ruler, playhead and zoom slider.

- **Ruler**: Indicates the position and length of the region selected in the Tracks area, or in the Project Audio Browser.

- **Info display**: Displays the start point and length of the selected area.

- **Waveform overview**: Displays a miniature view of the entire audio waveform.

- **Waveform display**: Provides a detailed view of the area selected in the waveform overview.

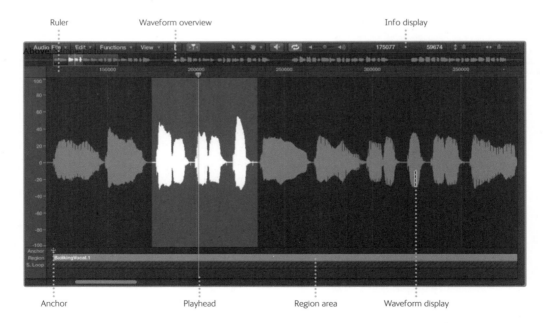

○ **Playhead**: Reflects the current playback position.

○ **Anchor**: Displays the absolute start point of the audio file.

○ **Region area**: Edit this beam to adjust the region length.

# LIST EDITORS

Here is a summary of the main List Editors and how to use them.

## Event List

The Event List shows all the events in your project, such as MIDI note events or region start events, in a vertical list format. You can use it to make precise edits and for other tasks better suited to numeric rather than graphic edits. You can display all events or limit them by category.

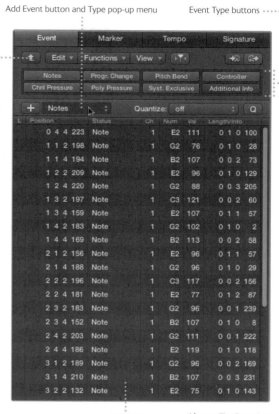

Add Event button and Type pop-up menu

Event Type buttons

Display Level button

List area

**Above:** The Event List.

○ **Display Level button**: Click to move up one display level in the Event List. This view lets you see all regions in the current project.

○ **Add Event button and Type pop-up menu**: Add an event, and choose the type of event to add.

○ **Event Type buttons**: Click to show or hide specific event types.

○ **List area**: Shows the list of events or regions, organized in columns.

## Marker List

The Marker List displays all the markers in the project. You can create, select and edit markers in the Marker List, and click a marker name to move the playhead to that marker position.

○ **Create button**: Creates a marker at the playhead position.

○ **Marker List area**: Lists all the markers in your project, showing the name, bar position and length of each marker. Drag vertically in the Position column to edit a marker's position, or double-click and enter a new value.

○ **Marker Text Area button**: Shows or hides the Marker Text area. Use this area to enter or edit text for the selected marker.

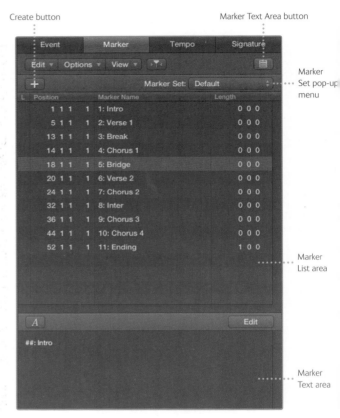

Create button

Marker Text Area button

Marker Set pop-up menu

Marker List area

Marker Text area

**Above**: The Marker List.

○ **Marker Text area**: Enter text for the selected marker by double-clicking the area or clicking the Marker Text Area button.

○ **Marker Set pop-up menu**: Choose the marker set to view and edit.

## Tempo List

The Tempo List displays all the tempo events in the project, and lets you create and edit tempo events.

- **Create button**: Click to create a new tempo event.

- **Tempo List area**: Displays all tempo changes and their position in a project.

- **Tempo Set pop-up menu**: Choose the tempo set to view and edit.

## Signature List

The Signature List shows all the time and key signature changes in your project, as well as any score symbols in the project score. You can create, copy, move and delete time and key signature events here.

- **Create button**: Click to create a new signature event.

- **Signature List area**: Displays all time and key signature changes and their positions.

- **Signature Set pop-up menu**: Choose the signature set to view and edit.

Create button    **Below**: The Tempo List.

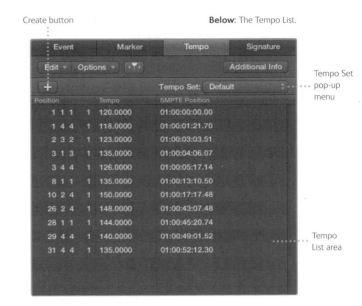

Tempo Set pop-up menu

Tempo List area

Create button    **Below**: The Signature List.

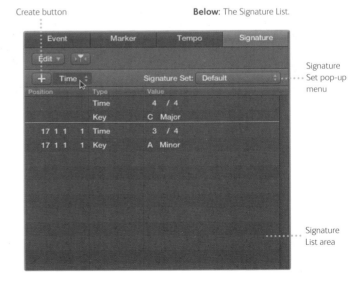

Signature Set pop-up menu

Signature List area

# ADVANCED TOOLS AND ADDITIONAL OPTIONS

**In Logic Pro, you can turn some advanced features on or off to suit your way of working.**

## SHOW ADVANCED TOOLS

When you turn on Show Advanced Tools, Logic Pro's full music production capabilities become available. All windows, views, menus and key commands required for standard music production tasks are accessible in the application. To turn on Show Advanced Tools:

1. Choose Logic Pro > Preferences > Advanced.    2.  Select the Show Advanced Tools checkbox.

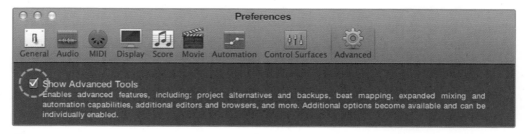

**Above:** Many important options are enabled by selecting Show Advanced Tools in the Advanced section of the Preferences window.

## ADDITIONAL OPTIONS

The Additional Options preference gives you access to extra capabilities for special tasks beyond the needs of usual music productions. When Show Advanced Tools is selected in the Advanced Preferences pane, the following additional options are available:

- **Audio:** Use the Audio File Editor for destructive editing of audio files and advanced configuration options.

○ **Surround**: Use surround capabilities (in the Mixer) with a surround setup.

○ **MIDI**: Use the Environment (a technical MIDI setup area) for MIDI signal flow control and real-time processing of MIDI data.

○ **Score**: Use additional features in the Score Editor, including the ability to assign staff styles to individual regions and create chord grids.

○ **Control Surfaces**: Create and edit control surface assignments.

○ **Advanced Editing**: Use advanced editing functions, including the Tempo Interpreter, and create aliases.

**Hot Tip**

For existing Logic Pro users upgrading to Logic Pro X, Show Advanced Tools and all additional options are turned on by default.

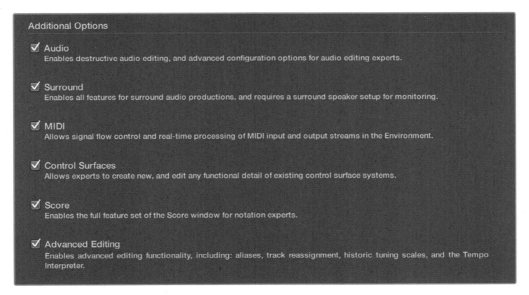

**Additional Options**

☑ **Audio**
Enables destructive audio editing, and advanced configuration options for audio editing experts.

☑ **Surround**
Enables all features for surround audio productions, and requires a surround speaker setup for monitoring.

☑ **MIDI**
Allows signal flow control and real-time processing of MIDI input and output streams in the Environment.

☑ **Control Surfaces**
Allows experts to create new, and edit any functional detail of existing control surface systems.

☑ **Score**
Enables the full feature set of the Score window for notation experts.

☑ **Advanced Editing**
Enables advanced editing functionality, including: aliases, track reassignment, historic tuning scales, and the Tempo Interpreter.

**Above**: The Additional Options section of the Advanced Preferences window enables extra capabilities for special tasks.

MIXING WITH LOGIC PRO

# MIXING WITH LOGIC PRO X

Logic Pro has a mixing window that graphically resembles the top of a
traditional analog mixing console. The Mixer window is a tried and true
way to see your work at a glance. This section will help you understand its
main functions and get you started toward creating your master mix!

## MIXING BASICS

When you mix a project, you balance its different parts and blend them into a cohesive whole.
You can also add effects to alter the sound, use routing and grouping to control the signal flow,
and use automation to create dynamic changes in your project over time. This is done in the
Mixer, which opens below the Tracks area or as a separate window.

**Below:** The Mixer window in Logic Pro X.

**Above:** There are no hard and fast rules where mixing is concerned – the more you do it, the better you become.

## What Does Mixing Involve?

Although there are no rules for mixing – except those learned from experience and a good ear – mixing typically involves the following steps, but not necessarily in the following order.

1.  Set channel strip volume levels to balance different instruments.

2.  Set channel strip pan, or balance, positions to place instruments in the stereo field.

For more on mixing, see Flame Tree's title *Mixing for Computer Musicians* by Ronan Macdonald.

3. Add and adjust effects and instruments to change the sound characteristics of individual tracks or the overall project.

4. Control signal flow to create subgroups, route signals to multiple destinations, or process sounds individually.

5. Create changes over time using automation curves on individual tracks or the master track.

In the process of mixing, you will find different ways to accelerate and simplify your workflow, by muting and soloing channel strips, working with channel strip groups, and customizing the Mixer.

## MIXER VIEWS

You can choose between different Mixer views when Show Advanced Tools is selected in the Advanced Preferences pane, displaying only those channel strips that you actually need for the mixing task at hand.

### Open the Mixer in the Main Window

There are two ways to open the Mixer in the main Window:

1. Click the Mixer button in the control bar.

2. Choose View > Show Mixer (or press X).

**Above:** Use the View buttons at the top of the Mixer window to select which channel strips to display.

## Open the Mixer as a Separate Window

Choose Window > Open Mixer (or press Command + 2).

## Choose a Different Mixer View

Do any of the following:

1. Click the Single button to show the signal flow of the channel strip that corresponds to the selected track in the Tracks area.

2. Click the Tracks button to show the signal flow of all channel strips that correspond to tracks used in the Tracks area.

3. Click the All button to show the signal flow of all channel strips available in the project.

**Above**: Pointing to the All button in the Mixer.

4. Use the Cycle Through Mixer Modes key command.

You can also perform some basic mixing tasks in the Tracks area.

# ALL ABOUT CHANNEL STRIPS

**Channel strips in Logic Pro X look and work just as they do on a physical mixer, and they appear in Logic's Mixer window. There are four types of channel strip: track, auxiliary (aux), output, and the master channel strip.**

## CHANNEL STRIP TYPES

You can display only those channel strips that you need for the task at hand. Here's a full description.

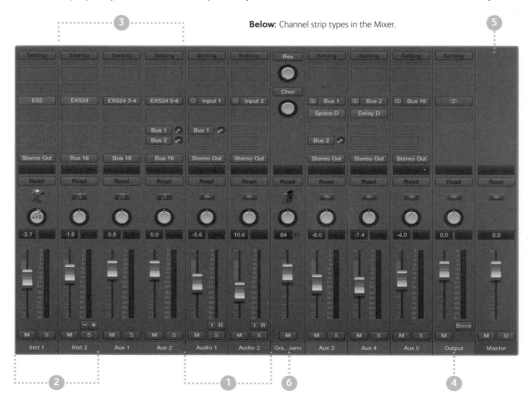

**Below:** Channel strip types in the Mixer.

1. **Audio channel strips:** These are used to control the playback and recording of audio signals on audio tracks. All data on the audio track is automatically routed to the audio channel strip assigned in the track list.

2. **Instrument channel strips:** These are used to control software instruments. Software instruments are inserted via the channel strip's Instrument slot. The instrument channel strip can then be driven by a recorded MIDI region, or by playing your MIDI keyboard.

3. **Aux (auxiliary) channel strips:** These are used for a variety of signal-routing purposes. Aux channel strips are used to set up send returns, where a channel strip signal is routed to an aux channel strip for effects processing. They are also used for grouping and for distributing a signal to multiple destinations via sends.

4. **Output channel strips:** These represent the physical audio outputs of your audio interface. They are used to adjust the overall level and stereo balance – or pan position, in the case of mono output channel strips – of all audio, instrument, or aux channel strips routed to them.

5. **Master channel strip:** Used as a global volume control for all output channel strips. The master channel strip changes the gain of all output channel strips without affecting the level relationships between them.

6. **MIDI channel strips:** Used to control external MIDI tracks. MIDI data on these tracks is routed to a MIDI output port and channel, for control of MIDI sound modules and keyboards.

**Hot Tip**

**Bus and input channel strips are included for compatibility with earlier versions of Logic Pro, but their functions are now handled by aux channel strips and audio channel strips.**

# CHANNEL STRIP CONTROLS

Each channel strip has a set of controls, depending on the type of channel strip. You can adjust the channel strip volume and pan position, mute and solo channel strips, add and adjust effects, and send the output to auxiliary or output channel strips.

1. **List Setting button**: Use to load, browse, or save channel strip settings for the selected track.

2. **Input/Instrument slot**: Choose the channel strip's input source – the physical audio interface input that your microphone or instrument is connected to.

3. **Audio Effect slot**: Inserts an audio effect into the channel strip. Use effects to alter signals in real time.

4. **Send slot**: Routes the signal to an aux channel strip. The Send Level knob that appears defines the amount of signal to route. Use sends to apply effects to multiple signals at the same time.

**Right:** Channel strip controls in the Mixer.

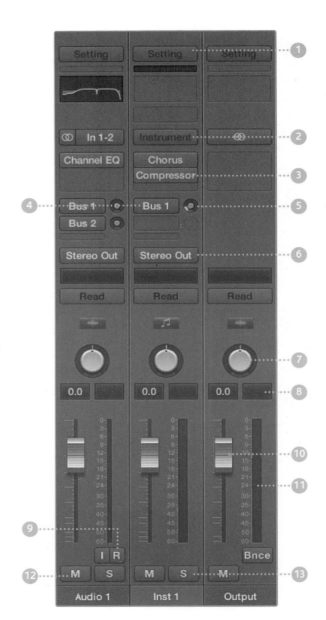

⑤ **Send Level knob:** Controls the amount of signal sent to an aux channel strip. Use sends to process effects for multiple signals at the same time.

⑥ **Output slot:** Choose where the channel strip's output signal is sent.

⑦ **Pan/Balance knob:** Sets the channel strip signal's position. On mono channel strips, it controls the signal's left/right position. On stereo channel strips, it controls the balance between the left and right signals.

⑧ **Peak level display:** Updates during playback to show the highest peak level reached. A red display indicates signal clipping.

⑨ **Volume display:** Shows the playback volume.

⑩ **Volume fader:** Adjusts the playback volume of the channel strip signal.

⑪ **Level meter:** Shows the level of the input signal – when playing an instrument or singing, for example. Amber and yellow signals are safe. Red indicates signal clipping.

⑫ **Mute button:** Removes the signal from the mix so that it can't be heard.

⑬ **Solo button:** Lets you hear the signal in isolation.

Other controls become available when Show Advanced Tools is selected in the Advanced Preferences pane.

# PEAK LEVEL DISPLAY AND SIGNAL CLIPPING

The Peak Level display is located above the Level meter. It updates during playback to show the peak level reached after the entire signal has been played through to the end. Use it to help set the Volume fader.

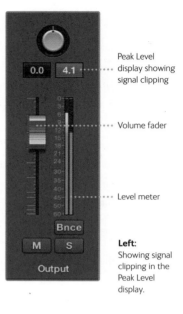

Peak Level display showing signal clipping

Volume fader

Level meter

**Left**: Showing signal clipping in the Peak Level display.

### Hot Tip

Individual channel strips can be safely clipped, as long as the output channel strip does not indicate clipping.

Signal clipping occurs when a signal that is too loud is fed through the output channel strip, thereby exceeding the limit of what can be accurately reproduced, resulting in distorted sound. The value shown in the Peak Level display lights red when the signal clips. This part of the Peak Level display is called the Clipping Indicator.

## Avoid Clipping

To avoid clipping, you need to bring down the Volume fader by the amount shown in red in the Peak Level display.

1.  Observe the value shown in the Peak Level display. In the screenshot, 1.7 dB is shown in the Peak Level display when the Volume fader is set to 2.2 dB.

2.  Drag the Volume fader down to a value of 0.5 or so. You may find that a Volume fader value of, say, -1.2 sounds best in the context of the overall mix, and clips only once (by 0.3 dB) during playback. If this is the case, it's nothing to worry about. Use your ears rather than your eyes as a guide.

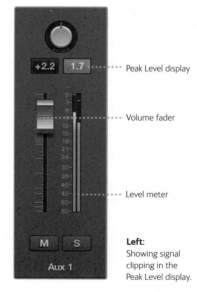

Peak Level display

Volume fader

Level meter

**Left**: Showing signal clipping in the Peak Level display.

# SET CHANNEL STRIP VOLUME LEVELS

You can set the volume level of each channel strip independently, balancing the relative volume of the tracks in your project. You can also quickly switch between two different volume levels on a channel strip.

## Setting the Volume Level

There are various ways to set a channel strip's volume level:

1. Drag the Volume fader up or down.

2. Option-click the Volume fader to return it to a neutral level (0 dB gain).

3. Hold down Shift while dragging the Volume fader to change the volume level in finer increments.

The Level meter, located to the right of the Volume fader, shows the channel strip output volume as the project plays. When you record, watch the Level meter to make sure the channel strip volume is not too high.

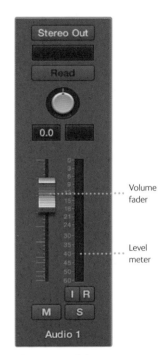

**Above:** Volume fader and Level meter.

## Set and Switch Between Two Different Volume Levels

1. Select an audio channel strip.

2. Drag the Volume fader to the level you want.

3. Use the Toggle Level of Audio Channel Strips key command. Note that the channel strip's Volume fader is all the way down.

4. Drag the Volume fader to a different level.

The Toggle Level of Audio Channel Strips key command now toggles between the two volume levels. It does so for all channel strips of the same type at once, allowing you to create two different mixes from one set of channel strips.

## CHANNEL STRIP INPUT FORMATS

The channel input format determines the configuration of the channel strip: mono, stereo, or surround. The symbol on the button indicates the current format:

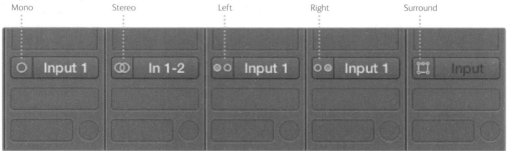

**Above:** Mono, stereo, left, right and surround input formats on channel strips.

- **Mono**: One circle represents the mono input format. The Level meter shows a single column.

- **Stereo**: Two interlocked circles represent the stereo input format. The Level meter divides into two independent columns when a stereo input format is chosen.

- **Left**: Two circles, with the left one filled, indicate the left channel input format. The left channel of a stereo audio file is played back. The Level meter shows one column.

- **Right**: Two circles, with the right one filled, indicate the right channel input format. The right channel of a stereo audio file is played. The Level meter shows one column.

- **Surround**: Five circles indicate the surround channel input format. The Level meter divides into multiple linked columns (the number matches the project surround format) when the surround input format is chosen.

# SET THE CHANNEL STRIP INPUT FORMAT

There are various ways to set the format of the channel strip input:

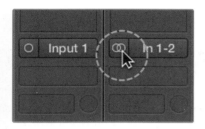

**Above:** Side-by-side of mono and stereo input format.

1. Click the Format button to switch between mono and stereo input format.

2. Click-hold the Format button, then choose an input format from the pop-up menu.

# SET THE CHANNEL STRIP PAN POSITION

You can separate parts of your mix by positioning audio and instruments in the stereo field from left to right. Typically, you want to have the most important tracks (lead vocals, solo instruments, drums, bass) positioned in the centre of the mix, and have other tracks (rhythm instruments, instruments doubling the melody) to the sides.

**Above:** This shows the Format pop-up menu open.

Pan knob

Balance knob

**Right:** Pan and Balance knobs.

The Pan knob defines whether a track is heard from the left, right, or centre of the stereo field. You can set the pan position for each track in a project. Mono channel strips feature a Pan knob, which determines the position of a signal in the stereo image. At the centre pan position, the channel strip sends equal amounts of the signal to both sides of the stereo image. Stereo channel strips feature a Balance knob, which differs from the Pan knob in that it controls the relative levels of two signals (left and right) at their outputs.

## Set a Channel Strip's Pan Position

There are various ways of setting a channel strip's pan position:

1. Drag the channel strip's Pan knob vertically or horizontally.

2. Option-click the Pan knob to return it to the centre position.

3. Hold down Shift while you drag the knob to change the pan position in finer increments.

**Hot Tip**

When a channel strip output is set to Surround, the Pan knob is replaced by a Surround knob.

## MUTE AND SOLO CHANNEL STRIPS

You can silence (mute) a channel strip so that you don't hear it. You can also listen to a channel strip signal in isolation (solo), silencing all other channel strips.

### Mute a Channel Strip

1. Click the channel strip's Mute button. The Mute button turns blue.

2. Click the button a second time to restore the channel strip to its previous level.

### Solo a Channel Strip

1. Click the channel strip's Solo button. The Solo button turns yellow.

**Above:** Pointing to the Mute button.

2. The Mute buttons of all unsoloed channel strips will flash blue, with the exception of external MIDI channel strips.

**Above:** Pointing to the Solo button.

## Solo a Second Channel Strip

To solo a second channel strip, option-click an unsoloed channel strip. This action solos the selected channel strip and unsolos any other channel strip.

## Disable the Solo State of One or More Channel Strips

1. Click an active Solo button.

2. Option-click any active Solo button. The solo state of all channel strips is deactivated.

**Above:** Showing a Solo button with a red slash to indicate solo-safe.

3. Control-click an inactive Solo button.

4. Make a channel strip solo-safe. A red slash across the Solo button indicates that the channel strip is solo-safe. The channel strip will not mute when you solo another channel strip. Control-click again to deactivate the channel strip's solo-safe state.

# USING PLUG-INS WITH LOGIC PRO X

Plug-ins are tiny programs that enhance your sequence or process your audio in various ways. Logic Pro X comes with a very useful assortment of these plug-ins, and the number you can purchase from third parties is almost endless.

## PLUG-IN TYPES

Plug-ins can be broken down into the following categories:

○ **Audio effects**: Can be inserted in audio, instrument, aux and output channel strips. Logic Pro offers a range of digital signal processing (DSP) effects and processors that are used to colour or tonally shape existing audio recordings, software instruments and external audio sources – in real time.

**Above:** Amp Designer is an example of an audio effects plug-in. You can choose different amp simulators to apply to a guitar or other audio track.

○ **MIDI effects**: Can only be inserted in instrument channel strips. Logic Pro offers easy access to real-time MIDI processing, which in previous versions of the software was only possible in the more technical MIDI setup area known as the Environment.

○ **Software instruments**: Can only be inserted in instrument channel strips. Logic Pro offers a range of software-based instruments that includes innovative synthesizers, a powerful sampler and authentic re-creations of vintage instruments that can be used in real time.

○ **GarageBand instruments**: Can only be inserted in instrument channel strips. GarageBand instruments are accessed by holding down Option when clicking an Instrument slot.

**Hot Tip**

Apple only supports 64-bit Audio Units' plug-ins in Logic Pro X. Some utilities from other companies may allow older 32-bit plug-ins in other formats (e.g. VST and RTAS).

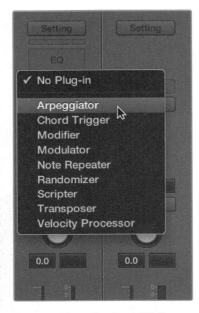

**Above:** Choosing a MIDI effect from the pop-up menu.

# ADD, REMOVE, MOVE AND COPY PLUG-INS

You can add plug-ins, replace a plug-in with a different one and remove plug-ins from a channel strip. You can also move, copy and bypass plug-ins.

## Add a MIDI Effect Plug-In

There are various ways to add a MIDI effect plug-in:

1. Click the MIDI Effect slot, then choose a plug-in from the pop-up menu.

2. Place the pointer above or below an occupied MIDI Effect slot, click the green line that appears, then choose a plug-in from the pop-up menu.

**Below:** Pointing to the green line under a MIDI Effect slot.

## Add an Audio Effect Plug-In

Choose from the following options to add an audio effect plug-in:

1. Click an Audio Effect slot, then choose a plug-in from the pop-up menu. The last visible empty Audio Effect slot in a channel strip is shown at half its height; use it in the same way.

2. Option-click an Audio Effect slot. You can now choose legacy plug-ins from the pop-up menu.

**Above:** Choosing an instrument from the pop-up menu.

## Add an Instrument Plug-In

There is more than one way to add an instrument plug-in:

1. Click the Instrument slot, then choose a plug-in from the pop-up menu.

2. Option-click an Instrument slot. You can now choose legacy plug-ins from the pop-up menu.

## For More on Plug-Ins

The quality and range of plug-ins is extensive and will make a world of difference to your mix. Check out the links at the end of the book for sites that offer plug-ins for Logic Pro X.

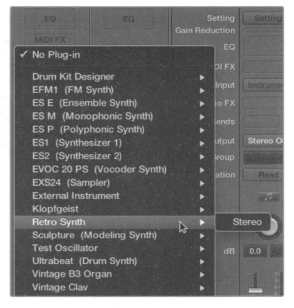

**Above:** Choosing an audio effect from the pop-up menu.

# AUTOMATION IN LOGIC PRO X

**You can record, edit and play back the movements of faders, knobs and switches in real time using automation. Each track in your project has automation curves for volume and pan, and you can add curves to automate plug-in settings. To create changes over time, follow these steps.**

## SHOW TRACK AUTOMATION CURVES

Before you can add control points to a track's automation curves, you need to show the track's curves. Automation curves are displayed on top of audio and MIDI regions across the track. Automation is represented by coloured curves and points.

**Above:** Showing track automation on for volume.

After you show the track's curves, choose which parameter you want to work with – Volume fader, Pan knob or other track parameter. You can work with multiple parameters on the same track or work in separate subtracks below the main track.

## CHOOSE AUTOMATION MODES

Automation modes determine how automation tracks are treated. Automation is either off, being read or being written. You can set the automation mode for each track.

○ **Off:** Hides any automation that exists on the track, without deleting it.

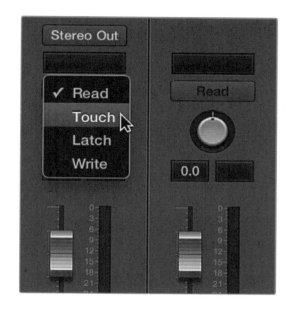

- **Read**: Plays back all automation that exists on the track. If volume data exists, for example, the Volume fader will move during playback following the prerecorded automation on the track. You can't change the value of the chosen automation parameter by moving controls when in Read mode.

- **Touch**: Plays back automation in the same way as Read mode. You can modify the value of the chosen automation parameter by moving controls in Touch mode. After the fader or knob is released, the parameter follows existing automation on the track.

- **Latch**: Works like Touch mode, but after the fader or knob is released, the new parameter value replaces existing automation on the track.

- **Write**: Erases existing automation on the track as the playhead passes over it. Records the new control movement or deletes the existing data if you do nothing.

**Above:** You can set the automation mode for each track. Automation is either off, being read or being written.

# WORKING WITH VIDEO AND MOVIES

You can use Logic Pro X to add audio to your movie. Making the audio work properly with the video is called synchronization.

## SYNCHRONIZATION

Logic Pro X supports most synchronization protocols, allowing you to work with external video and film-editing, and playback hardware. Logic Pro X Project video preferences are available when Advanced Tools and Additional Options are selected in the Advanced Preferences pane.

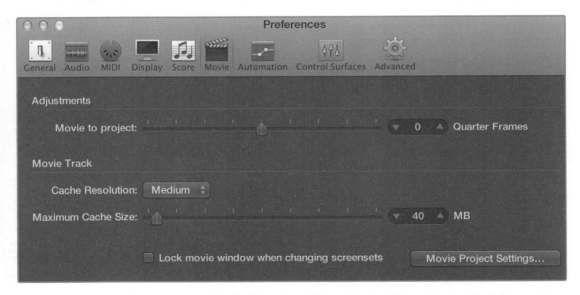

**Above**: Movie preferences are only available when Show Advanced Tools is selected in the Advanced section of the Preferences window.

# ADD A MOVIE TO YOUR PROJECT

You can view a QuickTime movie file synchronously with your project, making film and TV scoring quick and easy. Although you can't record or edit video directly in Logic Pro X, you can replace the soundtrack of a video file with music, effects and dialogue arranged in your project.

## Hot Tip

You will need a fast processor to ensure smooth movie playback. If you want to record and edit your own QuickTime movie from a video recorder or digital camera, you may need specialized hardware.

You can open a QuickTime movie in a separate Movie window and also display the single frames of a QuickTime movie in the global Video track.

**Above:** Main window showing a movie in global Video track, and also opened as a separate Movie window.

When a movie is opened in a project, the upper part of the inspector shows a closed Movie area, which can be opened by clicking the disclosure triangle.Movie playback follows the playhead position, and vice versa, in the Movie inspector area and in the Movie window. Audio playback for the movie is only audible if either the Movie inspector area or Movie window is open.

## Open a Movie Window in Logic Pro X
To open a Movie window, do any of the following:

1. Choose File > Open Movie (or use the corresponding key command, default assignment: Option + Command + O).

**Below:** You can open Movies quickly from the File menu.

2. Open the Movie pop-up menu in the global Movie track header, then choose Open Movie.

3. Click any position on the Video track with the Pencil tool.

4. Click the Media button in the control bar, then click the Movies button and choose the movie file.

The movie opens in the floating Movie window, in its correct aspect ratio. Only one QuickTime movie can be opened in a project. If you use the Open Movie command in a project that already contains a movie, a Movie window reopens with the same video clip.

## Remove a Movie from a Project

To remove a movie, choose either of these options, and all references to the movie will be deleted from the project.

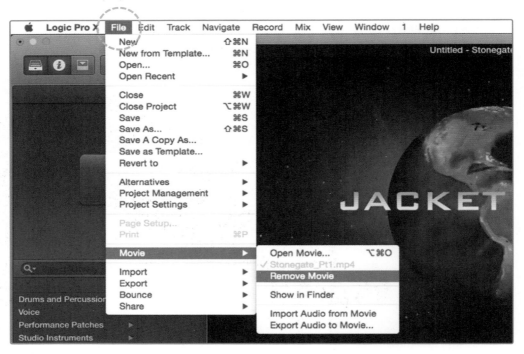

**Above:** You can remove movies from the File menu or the Media Browser window.

1. Choose File > Movie > Remove Movie (or use the corresponding key command).

2. Open the Movie pop-up menu in the global Movie track header, then choose Remove Movie.

# ABOUT THE MOVIE TRACK

The global Movie track displays the opened QuickTime movie as thumbnails. If the Movie track is not visible, set the preference Show and hide global tracks.

The number of frames displayed on the Movie track depends on both the track height and the zoom level of the window. All frames are aligned left, with only the very last frame aligned to the right. This guarantees that you can always see at least the first and last frames of a video, independent of the current zoom level. Given the left alignment of all frames (except the last), the left margin of a frame is always displayed at the exact position of that particular frame.

Movie track settings can be adjusted in the Movie preferences window.

## More About Mixing

In this section, we have just scratched the surface of the many amazing tools and features that let you build and fine-tune your mix in Logic Pro X. Be sure to take a look at the reading list at the back of the book for more resources and help files for Logic Pro.

**Below:** Video track showing movie frames displayed as thumbnails.

MASTERING WITH LOGIC PRO

# BOUNCING AND BURNING

**When you're done with your master mix, it's time to share it with the world, so here we'll look at how to put the final touches on your work for duplication on physical media or uploading to music sites.**

## ABOUT MASTERING

Mastering is the final step pro producers take to ensure their mix is of the highest quality and ready to play in whatever venue is appropriate. If you plan to release a CD's worth of music, mastering is essential to keeping tracks uniform in volume and consistent in tone as well as adding whatever degree of audio finish you'd like your tracks to have.

There are many mastering plug-ins available for Logic Pro X. You should also consider using a separate mastering engineer with fresh ears and mastering experience to evaluate your mix independently. If you use a separate facility for mastering, you can import the finished tracks back into Logic for distribution or further use.

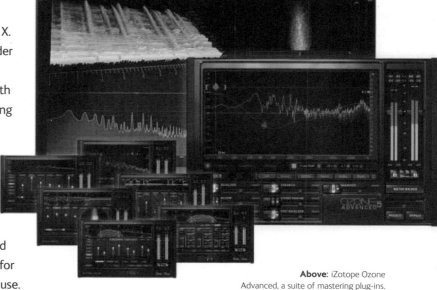

**Above:** iZotope Ozone Advanced, a suite of mastering plug-ins.

# FINAL MIX (BOUNCE) OPTIONS IN LOGIC PRO X

In Logic Pro X, you have various options for making your final mix available for sharing.

## Bounce a Project to an Audio File

You can render, or bounce, a project to a single audio file or to multiple audio files. A project can be bounced to several different PCM file formats simultaneously, including AIFF, Broadcast Wave, or CAF, as well as MP3 or MP4: AAC files, and a surround project can be bounced to a set of surround audio files.

**Above:** The Bounce settings dialog when PCM is selected as the destination.

Projects can be bounced either in real time or offline (which is typically faster). All parameters, effects and automation on the unmuted tracks in the project are recorded as part of the bounce file.

## Burn to a CD or DVD

In addition to bouncing a project to an audio file, you can burn the project to a CD or DVD (in DVD-Audio format). Logic Pro can directly burn Red Book audio to blank CDs or burn DVD-Audio to blank DVDs. You can bounce to one or more audio formats and burn the project to a disc at the same time.

## Other Bounce Options

You can also export an AAF file for use with Avid Pro Tools, export a project as an XML file for use with Final Cut Pro, or export a score as a MusicXML file for use with music notation applications.

# SHARING YOUR PROJECT

You can share a project to your iTunes library, to the Media Browser to use in other Apple applications, such as Final Cut Pro or iMovie, or to SoundCloud.

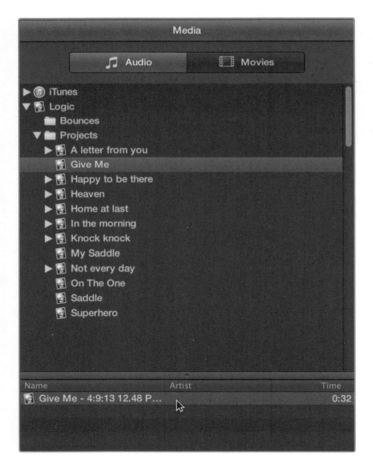

## Share the Project to Your iTunes Library

When you share a project to iTunes, the entire project, from the beginning to the end of the last region, is exported. Any silence at the beginning or end of the project is trimmed. If Cycle mode is on when you share the project, the part of the project between the start and the end of the cycle region is exported. Here is what to do:

1. Choose File > Share > To iTunes.

2. To rename the shared file, select the name in the Title field, then enter a new name.

**Left:** The Media Browser with the Audio tab selected, showing Logic projects.

**Above**: You can share an audio mix to your iTunes library or to another Logic Pro project.

3. Type artist, composer, and album information for the shared file in the text fields.

4. Choose the quality level for the shared file from the Quality pop-up menu.

5. Click Share.

The shared project appears in the iTunes library, where you can add it to playlists, convert it or burn it to a CD. The format of the shared project is determined by the iTunes import settings.

**Below**: If sharing to iTunes, your new mix with appear in your iTunes library.

## Share a Project to the Media Browser

The entire project, from the beginning to the end of the last region, is exported when you choose to share it to the Media Browser. Any silence at the beginning or the end of the project is trimmed. If Cycle mode is on when you share the project, the part of the project between the start and the end of the cycle region is exported.

1. Choose File > Share > To Media Browser.

2. To rename the shared file, select the name in the File name field, then enter a new name.

3. Type the artist, composer and album information for the shared file in the respective text fields.

4. Choose the quality setting for the shared file from the Quality pop-up menu.

5. Click Share.

## Share a Project to SoundCloud

If you have a SoundCloud account, you can share a project to SoundCloud. Make sure you choose the quality and visibility level, and set permissions for the shared project from within Logic Pro.

1. Choose File > Share > To SoundCloud.

2. If you aren't currently logged in to your SoundCloud account, enter your email address and password, then click Connect. Alternatively, you can log in to your Facebook account.

3. In the Share to SoundCloud dialog, do the following:

   ○ To sign in to a different SoundCloud account, click Change, then enter the login information for the account.

- To share the current project, select Bounce as the Source.

- To share an audio file, select File as the Source, click Browse, and then browse to the location of the file.

- Type the title, artist, composer and album information for the project in the respective text fields. Projects must have a title in the Title field. The remaining information is optional.

- Choose the quality level for the project from the Quality pop-up menu.

**Above**: The Share to SoundCloud dialog box with options.

- Choose the visibility level for the project from the Visibility pop-up menu.

- Set download and streaming permissions for the project in the Permissions section.

**4.** Click Share.

To return to Logic Pro without sharing the project, click Close.

# RECORD, MIX, SHARE, REPEAT

These techniques for sharing, like all the features and strategies described in this book, simply give you a springboard for diving into Logic Pro X and starting to make music. As you face challenges in achieving that perfect sound, you will learn all the amazing capabilities that Logic gives you, many of which were pipe dreams to producers a few short years ago.

# USEFUL WEBSITES AND FURTHER READING

## WEBSITES

https://www.apple.com/logic-pro
The official website for Logic Pro X with news, tutorials, plug-ins and sounds, testimonials and endorsers, and technical details.

https://www.gearslutz.com/board/logic-pro-x
One of the most extensive forums for Logic Pro X users.

http://logic-pro-expert.com
Extensive collection of gear reviews, tips, deals and information about Logic Pro.

http://www.logicprohelp.com
Links to free active forum and paid tutorials by Apple-certified trainers.

http://www.logicprokeycommands.com/logic-pro-x-key-commands/
All about keyboard shortcuts for Logic Pro X.

http://www.macprovideo.com/logic
Premium video tutorials.

http://music.tutsplus.com/tutorials/handy-shortcuts-for-logic-pro-x--cms-21621
A handy selection of shortcuts for Logic Pro X.

http://www.logic-cafe.com
Links to tutorials, blogs, downloads and shopping, all geared to Logic Pro.

## FURTHER READING

Anker, Kevin, *Logic Pro X Power!: The Comprehensive Guide*, Cengage, 2014

Cousins, Mark and Russ Hepworth-Sawyer, *Logic Pro X: Audio and Music Production*, CRC Press, 2014

Dvorin, David and Robert Brock, *Apple Pro Training Series: Logic Pro 9 Advanced Music Production*, Peachpit, 2014

English, Graham, *Logic Pro X For Dummies*, Wiley, 2014

Nahmani, David, *Apple Pro Training Series: Logic Pro X: Professional Music Production*, Peachpit Press, 2013

Rothermich, Edgar, *Logic Pro X – How It Works: A New Type of Manual – The Visual Approach*, Createspace Independent Publishing, 2014

# INDEX